Talking Your Way
to the Top

An Avant® Leadership Guide

Talking Your Way
to the Top

John W. Osborne

Avant Books®
San Marcos, California

Library of Congress Catalog Card Number: 89-43612

ISBN: 0-932238-48-3

Avant Books ®
Slawson Communications, Inc.
165 Vallecitos de Oro
San Marcos, CA 92069

Printed in the United States

Interior Design by Sandy Mewshaw
Cover Design by Lorri Maida
Artwork by Estay Heustis

10 9 8 7 6 5 4 3 2 1

Contents

Introduction

The ability to communicate is a prerequisite in today's competitive business climate. Successful businesses compete for people who can communicate ideas to others. The individual who speaks effectively before groups, conducts efficient meetings, and generates a good impression on camera is the one others look to for leadership. Business people who demonstrate this ability learn that the skill of public speaking is a direct link to promotion.

Many allow the fear of speaking in public to hold them back, while others who are good speakers and presenters take advantage of opportunities and move ahead. This book provides a strategy for quickly overcoming fear and gives the essential information necessary to succeed as a speaker.

Chapter 1

Overcoming Fear

Developing
Self-Confidence

A major obstacle for those on their way to the top is often the fear of public speaking. If you believe your fear is unique because you suffer strong feelings of mental and physical discomfort, you are wrong! Your fear is normal, almost all professional performers and entertainers experience it.

On a trip to New York I was seated next to Helen Hayes. Knowing that she had the reputation of being the "First lady of the American theater," I couldn't resist asking if she ever experienced nervousness when speaking in front of an audience. I was surprised to hear her reply, "Oh yes, many times. I just gave a presentation at the Beverly Hills Hotel for a women's group and I was so nervous–but that's enough talk about my stage fright."

It was hard to believe that a professional who has years of experience performing on Broadway and in motion pictures continues to feel nervousness when called upon to speak. By the time the plane landed at Kennedy, Ms Hayes had convinced me that performers never eliminate fear entirely, "They just train hard and learn to control it."

Antidote for Fear is a Positive Attitude

If you list the fears that afflict you as a speaker, you will understand that the problem is less serious than you thought. The fears you feel may include:

- Physical fear of the audience.

- Fear of ridicule.

- Fear of making a spectacle of yourself.

- Fear that what you may have to say is not worth saying.

- Fear that you may bore the audience.

Fear of the audience is a mental attitude. It can be replaced with confidence, another mental attitude.

How Mental Attitudes are Formed

Attitudes are formed out of our past experiences and have much to do with our beliefs and feelings. An attitude is a subconscious reaction to a situation. It determines how we will react in a given set of circumstances. An attitude can be favorable, "I enjoy public speaking" or negative, "I can't stand it."

You were not born with attitudes, they were programmed from past experiences. If the thought of speaking before a group terrifies you, then you may have had a bad speaking experience as a child. The event may have subjected you to criticism or ridicule by your peers, teachers, or parents, resulting in a negative impact on your self-image.

Attitudes Reflect Self-Esteem

The self-image is the core of human personality, and it regulates your performance within any given area. It is the internal picture of yourself. Your self-image is a composite of all your beliefs about yourself and these are based upon your interpretation of all past experiences.

How you feel about your self-image determines your self-esteem. Your self-esteem is displayed to others by your attitude. If you have high self-esteem in the area of public speaking, you will demonstrate a positive attitude when asked to speak in public, and approach the occasion with confidence and poise. If you are a low self-esteem speaker, you are fearful and show nervousness because you are performing outside of your comfort zone.

The Comfort Zone

Your comfort zone is that zone which corresponds with the self-image in any particular area of your life. You effectively and efficiently perform tasks and skills in this area. Performing outside this zone lowers your performance and causes anxiety and stress. Your self-image and corresponding comfort zone work like a regulating mechanism. Just as a thermostat controls room temperature by sending electrical impulses to start or stop the heater *when the room falls below or rises above the desired temperature*, we as human beings are controlled by tension *when we move either too far above or below our self-image*. The self-image is the subconscious picture–or thermostat setting–of how we see ourselves. It regulates our behavior by allowing us to move above or below our current self-image only slightly, thus defining our comfort zone. Moving too far above or below our comfort zone causes stress and anxiety. Here is how it works:

Example: Public Speaking

Your Self-Image:	Based upon past experiences you see yourself as a poor speaker.
Your Self-Esteem:	You feel bad about being a poor speaker and you have a negative attitude about speaking in public.
Your Comfort Zone:	Speaking before groups puts you outside your comfort zone.
Your Performance:	When you speak or make a presentation, you are not acting within your subconscious image of yourself. Your subconscious becomes very uncomfortable and transfers this feeling to the conscious through anxiety and fear.
The Result:	Your subconscious inhibits your performance by eroding your poise and confidence. Your voice cracks and you can't think of what to say.
What You Say to Yourself (Self-Talk):	You reaffirm that you knew you would do poorly because you always do. That is just like you.

Because of your beliefs about yourself, your subconscious mind forms a comfort zone that automatically controls your behavior to conform with your version of your performance reality. The action is an automatic subconscious check and balance control system. Once outside of your comfort zone, you develop a burning desire to get back to where your self-image makes you feel at ease–where you belong.

If your goal is to overcome your fear of speaking before groups you must enlarge your comfort zone. This requires changing your self-image (Figure 1.1).

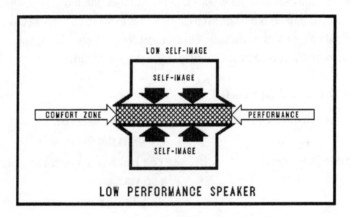

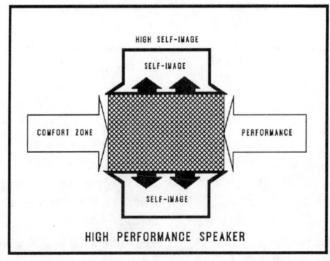

Figure 1.1   Self-Image Controls Performance

Self-Talk Builds the Self-Image

Self-talk is the conversation you carry on with yourself. It is the self-talk that accumulates on the subconscious level, that builds your self-image or belief system. If you can control the quality and quantity of self-talk information that is programmed into your subconscious, you can build your self-image and upgrade your self-esteem. As attitudes are originated from the self-image, your self-image is a product of your self-talk. So to the degree that your self-talk is constructive, expanding and self-complimenting, you are building within yourself a belief system that is positive, confident and constructive.

Present Thoughts Determine Your Success

Your present thoughts determine your future success. The way you talk to yourself forms an image, and the image you hold in your mind draws your subconscious toward the picture you create for yourself. While you visualize success as being confident and effectively speaking in front of a group, you will unconsciously move yourself in that direction. Visualize yourself speaking in public and inevitably you will move toward that goal (Figure 1.2).

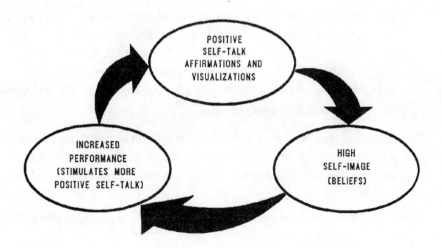

Figure 1.2   Positive Self-Talk Cycle

Develop a Personal Program

To become a confident and effective speaker you must develop a personal program that provides actual speaking experience and the opportunity to apply the knowledge provided in this book. Your program will be your strategic approach for developing confidence and expertise, step by step, from the simple to the complex, learning and gaining experience at your own pace. Your strategy should look like this:

Strategy for Becoming an Effective Speaker

- Join a Toastmaster Club or enroll in a company sponsored speech or presentation training class. This will provide you with actual speaking experience in front of a live audience.

- Train and practice at home with a video camera and recorder. Working with video, you can learn at your own pace by starting with one sentence and expanding your presentation to thirty minutes. As you see yourself develop on camera, you will literally feel your self-esteem growing.

- Speak at every opportunity. Be on the lookout for appropriate speaking opportunities that will add to your experience and confidence. An example is making a toast at dinner among friends.

- Use positive self-talk and visualization daily. Listen to what you say to yourself. Eliminate the word "can't" from your vocabulary. Develop a "can do" mental set and concentrate on the positive. Tell yourself, "I can," "I will," "I am succeeding." Pick a positive, affirming message and repeat it daily for at least twenty-one days. If a negative thought pops up, immediately find a positive antidote and consciously repeat it.

- Speak and act as a professional. Speak and act with authority, confidence, and energy, even if you don't completely believe it, yet. Your beliefs, self-image, self-esteem and comfort zone will eventually expand to coincide with your new picture.

Once you have formulated your speaking strategy, you are ready to proceed with learning the public speaking essentials.

Chapter 2

Presentation Preparation

Before we look at presentation preparation, there are some communication facts you need to know.

Non-Verbal Elements

Verbal communication contains non-verbal elements. Research has revealed that communication goes far beyond words. Only seven percent of interpersonal communication is traceable to words and the rest is contained in non-verbal elements. About fifty-five percent is the result of facial expression and other body language and thirty-eight percent comes from how we use our voices. Research also tells us presentations are more effective if they contain visual materials.

Listener Retention

The typical listener will remember only about ten percent of a presentation one week after hearing what was presented. Within half an hour, the average listener will forget forty percent of what was said. By the end of the day, sixty percent will be forgotten.

An experienced speaker will design his or her presentation to increase retention by:

- Repetition   – The more frequently a message is heard, the more likely it is to be remembered.

- Proximity   – The more recently a message is heard, the better it will be re-membered.

- Impression   – The greater the impression or emotional impact upon the lis-tener the longer the message will be remembered.

- Simplicity   – A simple presentation is easy to understand.

Preparing An Effective Presentation

Successful presentations are built upon a solid foundation of extensive preparation. Most presentations fail because of poor or inadequate preparation. A good rule of thumb for beginning speakers is to allow two hours of preparation for every minute of speaking time. This may sound excessive but you can't be too well prepared. Preparation time will decrease with experience. One of the secrets of your success as a speaker is that you will have prepared the right presentation for the right audience at the right time and you will have a back-up plan if something goes wrong.

Seven Steps in Preparing an Effective Presentation

Preparing an effective presentation can be reduced to a few basic steps. All of these steps, described below, should be reviewed and systematically followed.

Step 1:   Establish Objectives for the Presentation

Ask yourself the question, "Why am I giving this presentation?" and not, "What am I going to put into it?"

Most presentation goals will consist of one or more of the following:

- To Sell
- To Inform
- To Educate
- To Motivate
- To Create Action
- To Entertain
- To Commemorate

When you establish your goal, decide what will be the measure of a successful presentation. You must establish what the desired end result will be. It must be realistic and achievable.

Step 2: Analyze Your Audience.

Identify the specific audience in terms of knowledge, attitudes, likes, and dislikes, as a guide to determine which facts and approach are most likely to be effective in achieving your objectives.

Basic demographic information can help plan your approach and the type of material to use. These demographics include:

- Age
- Sex
- Income Level
- Occupation or Professional Status
- Political Affiliation
- Ethnic Identity

Information about your audience can be obtained by:

- Questioning other people who have spoken to this audience.

- Learning more about the company or organization to which this audience belongs.

- Reviewing reports from, or about, members of the audience.

- Inquiring directly or indirectly from selected members of the audience or others associated with them.

- Thinking logically and applying common sense to what you already know about the situation and the audience.

All audiences want to hear audience-centered messages that reflect their needs, values and beliefs. To ensure success with any audience, you must design your presentation to give them the following messages:

- I Will Not Waste Your Time - Audiences get upset when they sense their time is being wasted.

- I Know Who You Are - A speaker must address the audience's needs and interests.

- I Am Well Organized - The message must be clear and easily understood.

- I Know My Subject - Audiences want speakers who possess high levels of expertise and speak with authority.

- Here is My Most Important Point - It is the speaker's responsibility to make the audience understand why they are there.

- I Am Finished - The speaker must bring it all together and provide a solid finish or the audience will feel cheated.

Step 3:   Prepare a Presentation Plan

The Presentation Plan is like a blueprint (Figure 2.1). It helps you build a framework on which to develop a presentation, and it helps you decide how much and what kind of material you will need. It also serves as a guide for support personnel who provide back-up data, prepare visual aids, or who assist in the presentation staging (art department, graphic services, audio visual department, etc.). The plan is not designed to be a speaking outline, but a conceptual approach to what will most logically lead you to accomplish your objectives.

Step 4:   Select Resource Material

Finding sufficient resource material is not generally a problem. The problem is one of proper selection. You must determine what and how much of the available material should be included in the presentation.

There is no magic formula that will guarantee proper selection, but here are some common sense questions that may help.

- What is the object or purpose of the presentation?

- What should be covered? What can be eliminated?

- What amount of detail is necessary?

- What must be said if the objectives are to be reached?

- What is the best way to say it?

- What kind of audience reaction or response is required if the objectives are to be met?

Finally, submit all resource material to the "why?" test. If you cannot justify that the material selected contributes to the achievement of objectives, eliminate it.

Presentation Plan

Presentation	Subject: _____ Location: _____ Requestor:
Presentation Objectives	Desired Results: _____ _____ _____
Audience Analysis	Audience Demographics: _____ Audience Appeals: _____ Audience Needs: _____ Audience Beliefs: _____ _____ _____
Physical Arrangements	Room Reservations & Set-up: _____ Refreshments: _____ Support Personnel: _____ _____ _____ _____
Audio-Visual Requirements	Visual Aids / Graphics Services: _____ Equipment: _____ Set-up: _____ Support Personnel: _____ _____ _____ _____
Presentation Content	Presentation Organizational Style: _____ Main Idea or Concept: _____ _____ _____ _____
Research Requirements	Reports, Studies, Facts, Statistics, etc.: _____ _____ _____
Question & Answer Session	Sensitive Issues: _____ Difficult Questions: _____ _____ _____
Back-up Plan	Alternate Method of Presenting Message: _____ _____

Figure 2.1 Presentation Plan

Step 5:   Organize Your Material

This represents the presentation outline which incorporates selected material into a format that will fit your style, meet the objectives, and satisfy the needs of the audience. The three distinct parts to a well organized presentation are:

Introduction - *Tell them what you are going to tell them.* Be brief. The purpose of the introduction is to:

- Sell the audience on listening to the presentation.

- Introduce the subject or purpose of the presentation.

Body - *Tell them.* Develop and support your idea with selected material. The body should:

- Follow the main ideas listed in the presentation plan and identify and interpret these ideas in a manner which will be meaningful to the audience.

- Handle the audience's questions and/or discussions. This can be the most crucial part of the presentation. Careful thought should be given to when and how this will be done.

Conclusion - *Tell them what you told them.* This should be the strongest part of your presentation and should:

- Provide a summary of main ideas and objectives.

- Appeal directly for action, belief or understanding.

- Review vividly the idea or purpose of the entire presentation.

Presentation organization will be discussed in greater detail in the next chapter.

Step 6:   Practice the Presentation

Preparation of a presentation is not complete until you have rehearsed it in a practice session. Practice will help assure success, but it will not make a good presentation out of one that is poorly planned or disorganized. Practice will:

- Give you more self-confidence and poise, resulting in the audience being more willing to place credence in the subject matter.

- Identify flaws or gaps in the material.

- Provide familiarity with the material so that the right words come naturally and spontaneously.

- Allow you to utilize the visual aids so that they will strengthen, not interfere with, the actual presentation.

- Make it easier to anticipate potential questions, particularly ones that might prove troublesome.

There are three primary methods of practicing the presentation before actually presenting it:

- Give the presentation aloud to yourself.

- Use a recorder, audio or video.

- Give a dry run before some knowledgeable co-workers, friends, or even some representative members of your design audience.

Step 7:   Prepare a Back-up Plan

Preparing a back-up plan is an important step, because your presentation may not go as planned. As a speaker, there are things outside of your direct control that can go wrong. Depending on the type of presentation you are giving, some problems you may encounter are:

- Visual aids problems.

- Audio visual equipment failure.

- Facilities power failure.

- Illness of support personnel.

- Unexpected interruptions.

- Lose train of thought or *freeze* during the presentation.

You can't anticipate every problem and you shouldn't try. The important point is to recognize that something serious could go wrong and you must have a fall-back position. This means that in the worst of circumstances you should have a back-up plan ready that will enable you to deliver your message to the audience. The plan should include an Introduction, Body, and Conclusion. It should be written and kept available during the presentation to be used as notes and, if necessary, read (Figure 2.2).

Back-Up Plan
(Parachute)

Presentation Title: _____

Introduction/Opening Line: _____

_____

_____

Body/Main Points:

   1.

   2.

   3.

Conclusion/Closing Line: _____

_____

_____

Figure 2.2 Back-up Plan

Preparation Summary

Each of seven steps has a separate and distinct contribution to make and none of them should be overlooked. In summary they are:

1. **Establish the objectives** for your presentation. Determine why you are giving the presentation and what you hope to accomplish.

2. **Analyze your audience** in terms of their knowledge, attitudes and ability to act. Keep this information in mind as you prepare the presentation.

3. **Prepare a Preliminary Plan** concentrating on the main ideas or concepts the audience must understand if your objectives are to be met.

4. **Select the resource material** for your presentation, following your Preliminary Plan. Be prepared to justify the inclusion of each item in terms of your objectives.

5. **Organize your material** in a logical and effective manner for your audience, putting particular effort into a strong introduction and conclusion.

6.   **Practice your presentation** before you meet your audience. Get the bugs out of the presentation so you can present it as smoothly as possible.

7.   **Prepare a back-up plan** in the event that your presentation does not go according to plan.

If you systematically follow these seven preparation steps you will experience the following results:

- Increased self-confidence.

- Reduction of twenty to fifty percent in preparation time.

- Reduction of more than fifty percent in presentation time.

- Substantial reduction in the number and complexity of visual aids.

- Increased audience reception.

Now that you understand the process of how to prepare your presentation, let's look at how presentations can be organized.

Chapter 3

Organizing The Presentation

An effective presentation is logically organized into an opening, a body, and a conclusion. There are many variations on this structure but all three are present in a good speech. After you have completed your presentation plan, you should begin to mentally organize your talk. Write an outline to be certain each of these three points is included in your presentation and mentally visualize each point clearly. Give special attention to your conclusion so you know where your presentation is headed.

Opening - Catch Their Attention

Attention is a prerequisite to communication. The more audience attention you can get, the more communicating you can accomplish.

The opening of your presentation must be designed to catch immediate attention. It should arouse the audience's interest in your topic and alert them to the theme of your talk. Your opening must also lead into a subject of the presentation. If you merely shock the audience, they will remember the opening clearly, but forget the point of the talk. Examples of a good opening are:

- A startling question or a challenging statement.

- An appropriate quotation, illustration, or story.

- A display of some appropriate object or picture.

- A generalization that focuses attention and ties in with your subject.

When preparing your opening, be sure to avoid these common weaknesses:

- An apologetic statement.

- A story that does not relate to your topic.

- A commonplace observation delivered in a commonplace manner.

- A long or slow moving statement.

- A trite question, such as "Did you ever stop to think . . . ?"

Once you have decided on the opening, it must be committed to memory. The first moments before the audience are critical in making a good impression. You want to maximize that time and your interaction by using all of your energy in projecting the message and producing good audience contact.

Body - Support Your Purpose

The body of your presentation contains the factual support for your purpose. The amount of information you can include in the body will be limited by the amount of time available. The type of information in your talk will depend on your presentation goal and style. The presentation body can include:

- **Research** - The results of a careful systematic study and investigation in some field of knowledge.

- **Proof** - Evidence or fact that establishes the truth of something.

- **Evidence** - A statement of fact or personal testimony or documentation that furnishes proof.

- **Fact** - A statement that can be verified, either by referring to a third source or by direct observation.

- **Figure** - Numerical representation of a fact.

- **Statistic** - Expression of factual relationships based on counting.

- **Definition** - Inquiry into the nature of something, usually by identifying its particular qualities, e.g., "A man (term) is a type of mammal (general class) that walks upright, etc. (particular quality)."

- **Example** - A representation, story, or experience, included to illuminate but not necessarily to prove a point.

- **Illustration** - A more detailed example, offering point-by-point clarification.

- **Anecdote** - A representation, story, or experience can be included to illuminate, but not necessarily to prove a point.

- **Authority** - A citation from a reliable, recognized source in support of the speaker's point.

- **Analogy** - A set of parallel conditions that by their similarity and familiarity throw light on what is being discussed.

Conclusion - Bring It All Together

The conclusion of your presentation is the climax–the destination at which you hope to leave your audience. This is where your speech should produce results. Your conclusion should always tie in with your opening and should leave no doubt about what you want your audience to do with the information. Finish forcefully and with confidence. A weak, inconclusive, apologetic closing will kill even the best presentation.

Examples of good closings are:

- A summary of the points you have made and the conclusions to be drawn from them.

- A specific appeal for action.

- A story, quotation, or illustration that emphasizes your point.

Organization Style

Even if you are using the best material possible, your presentation effectiveness will be lost if it is not properly outlined and organized. There are many ways to organize material for a presentation. Each person's mind forms its own unique patterns of exposition and persuasion, and to prescribe patterns is to oversimplify what may be crucial to the presenter's success. There are, nonetheless, several general patterns which have proven helpful in arranging materials:

- **Time/Sequence** - Events are presented in the sequence in which they occur. The chronological sequence gives a specific time context to the event.

- **Topical** - This type of pattern assigns meaningful labels to subtopics related to the general topic. It is most often used when the presenter cannot confine the topic to the procedure, a process or a time-frame. It is helpful where the presenter is exploring new ideas that have not yet been put into organizational understanding.

- **Question and Answer** - The presenter will ask a question or questions and then systematically provide the answer or answers.

- **Problem and Solution** - This pattern is commonly used in business and technical presentations where the speaker identifies a problem and then states what needs to be done to solve it. Often this pattern includes:

  1. Stating the symptoms of the problem to the audience to gain credibility that a problem exists.

  2. Identifying the real problem for analysis.

  3. Providing solutions including constraints on the solution.

  4. Recommending the best solution.

- **Contrast and Comparison** - Here the speaker's plan is to call the audience's attention to differences or similarities in order to get them to evaluate alternative ideas or plans.

- **Combinations** - Obviously, each of these patterns can be combined with another. As a presenter, your task is to develop the optimum combination in terms of your topic, your audience, and your objectives of informing and persuading.

More on Style

We have already looked at the basics of presentation, organization, and style. Now, we will take a closer look at three styles that have good business applications. All should be used at different times in constructing your presentations. They are all good and all can be adapted to different subjects. The characteristic they have in common is they lead the audience step-by-step from lack of knowledge or interest to an informed conclusion on the subject. The key phrase is *step by step*.

AIDA - Outline

The first variation on the basic *opening-body-conclusion* method is the AIDA outline. This approach is often taught to salespeople and it can be applied to anything you are selling, whether ideas, objects or action. The AIDA outline is:

A - Win their <u>A</u>ttention
I - Arouse their <u>I</u>nterest
D - Create a <u>D</u>esire
A - Stimulate <u>A</u>ction or Agreement

Borden - Listeners' Reactions

The second approach was designed by Richard C. Borden, a speech professor at New York University. Its four steps represent the listener's reactions to what you are saying.

1. "Ho-Hum."

   This corresponds to your introduction. The audience is sitting back, expecting to be bored. It is up to you to make them sit up and listen.

2. "Why bring that up?"

   You must build a bridge to carry the audience. Show that your subject is important and relate it directly to the interests of your listeners.

3. "For instance?"

   Give the audience concrete evidence, illustrations, facts, and stories. Start your listeners thinking.

4. "So what?"

   This is the call for action. Tell the audience what you want them to do as a result of your presentation. Be specific and finish forcefully.

Past / Present / Future - Outline

A third approach is the *past-present-future* outline that fits especially well with a talk on an historical subject or an examination of human development. You could use this outline for a speech on the growth of your business or profession, or the expansion of a business system. The outline might be used in this form:

- There was a time when . . .

- But today, things have changed. . .

- As we look into the future . . .

When you use any of these three suggestions, be sure to open with an attention getting statement (although not a sensational one). Immediately engage the audience's interest, showing why they should care about what you are saying. Then, in the body of the speech introduce your arguments and support each of them with facts and examples. Finally, present a conclusion that calls for some type of action by the listeners, whether physical or mental.

Chapter 4

Visual Aids

Even the most accomplished speaker can improve the presentation by using visual aids. Research conducted by the University of Minnesota and the 3M Corporation concluded that an audience is forty-three percent more likely to be persuaded by presenters who use visuals. Their skillful and moderate use can add polish to a presentation that no amount of extra speaking can contribute. A visual aid is designed to supplement a presentation by performing a specific function. It is not a crutch or substitute for the presentation itself.

When to Use Visual Aids

Visual aids can be used anywhere in the presentation to help get the message across. They can be used in the following manner:

- **In the opening,** to gain attention, to arouse interest, and to show the audience what you are going to present.

- **In the presentation body,** to provide evidence, and to provide visual material at points when audience interest and retention may be low.

- **In your conclusion,** to link with the opening, reinforce a memory, summarize your presentation and tie your presentation together.

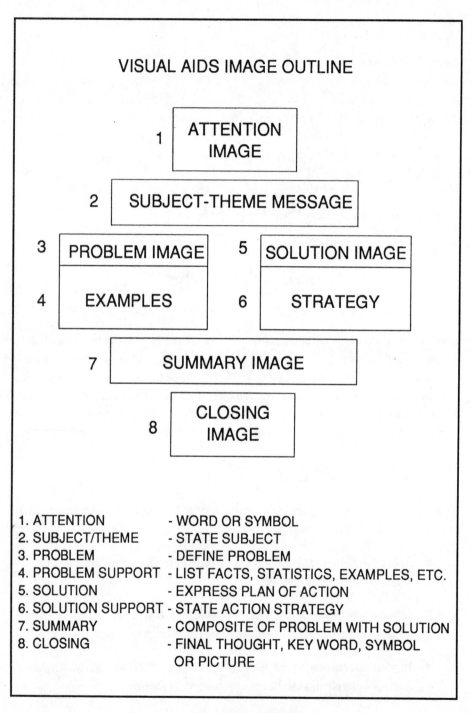

Figure 4.1   Visual Aids Image Outline

Visual Aids Image Outline

A quick and easy method that will help determine where to place visual aids is to construct an outline. A Visual Aid Image Outline is a flow chart diagram depicting the different parts of your presentation, and it illustrates where a visual aid can be used. It is derived from the Presentation Plan and Organization Style discussed in Chapter 2. If, for example, you were planning a presentation with a problem-solution-organization style, your visual aid outline would look something like the diagram (Figure 4.1).

Important Visual Aids Guidelines

Good visuals are simple. Like newspaper and magazine display advertisements, your charts, diagrams and graphics should be simple and to the point. Every item of information must relate to your main points or presentation goal.

As useful as visuals are, they should be used in moderation. Your audience is there to see and hear *you*, not your media show. Poorly planned and executed visuals can harm your presentation more than help. The cure for this is being prepared and following these simple guidelines:

- Limit each visual to one main idea.
- Use handouts to communicate detailed information.
- Visuals should be simple and to the point; include only information you plan to discuss.
- All writing, printing and diagrams should be large and legible.
- Avoid too much crowding.

Types of Visual Aids

The most effective type of visual aid to select for your graphics presentation depends on the size of the audience, the size of the room, the type of information to be presented visually, and the equipment available. The different kinds of visual aids are:

- Flip charts.
- Overhead projection.
- 35 mm slides.
- Film.
- Video monitors.

- Projection television.

- Cut-aways, mock-ups and props.

- Handouts.

Flip Chart

This is the most effective visual for an audience up to twenty-five people and is an excellent media to present simple text or graphics.

In planning your charts think of key words. Your audience sees the key word or phrase; you provide the explanation. A chart used to explain key words would look like this:

Key Words:
Emphasize
Strengthen
Captivate
Motivate

If you prefer to use complete sentences or if your presentation requires that you use complete sentences, do so, but be consistent and stick to one style. If you do the first item on a chart with a sentence, do the same for all the other items on that chart. An example of this style looks like this:

Making Intelligent Statements:
Use Simple Words.
Make All Words Count.
Form Simple Sentences.
Keep The Message Clear.

Prepare your charts in advance to allow time for proper organization and layout. Writing on a flip chart during your presentation creates a pause, and unless your addition to the chart is quite concise and relevant, this pause will be too long. This is not to say that you shouldn't write on your charts during your presentation, because you should! Research studies indicate that higher retention occurs if the chart is not completed beforehand. Completing or adding to the charts during the presentation provides an air of spontaneity, and watching the presenter in the art of creating the visual has special significance for the audience. It is an expression of you and your personality, not just prepackaged information or a canned presentation.

Overhead Projection

Overhead projection using transparencies is useful for displaying visuals to fifty people or less. Specialized equipment is needed to produce overhead transparencies, however, most of today's plain paper copiers will handle the job. The overhead projector is like any other piece of equipment and requires the following presentation preparation and set up:

- Be familiar with the equipment, controls, and operation.
- Check to ensure equipment is set up and operating properly.
- Check to see that there is a spare bulb on hand.
- Make a final check to ensure the projector is focused and will be ready to go when you are.

When using overhead projection it is tempting to begin and end your presentation with a visual; however, it may take away from your audience contact. They will be looking at the visual instead of giving you their full attention.

As with any visual, you should pause after displaying the overhead. Let the audience absorb the information before you begin to talk about it.

When discussing your graphics, step away from the projector and talk near the screen, remembering to face your audience.

When pointing to a piece of information on the screen, use either a pointer to point to the screen or a thin pen (or other thin implement) to lay directly on the transparency itself. Pointing your finger to the screen or transparency results in you or your hand being in front of the projection lamp, blocking most of the image that appears on the screen.

If you have a number of graphics to present, vary your presentation. Occasionally introduce material verbally before presenting the image, this technique helps to hold your audience's attention.

Photographic Color (35mm) Slides

Color slides are very effective for an audience of ten to several hundred people. Slides are an excellent medium because they present accurate pictures of people, places, objects, and events. However, careful design and execution are required to produce top quality results. Slides are more likely to be judged by professional standards than charts or overhead transparencies, and presenters usually do not use them unless they have access to quality material.

The main disadvantage with slides is the necessity to darken the room. This disrupts the continuity of the overall presentation and has a tendency to cause the presenter to group all visuals together. This may not work to the advantage of the presentation.

The main advantage of using slides is that they are simple to present. But, as with any projection system, you must rely on the electrical system, so check out the equipment in advance. If the system fails, be prepared to go on without it.

Film, Video Monitors and Projection Television

Film and video work well for certain types of presentations. Films and projection television can be shown to any size audience. Video monitors are useful for up to twenty-five people per monitor. Video is becoming increasingly popular with the use of on-line computer output and the increased use of computer graphics.

When using film and video-type playback, you need to pay special attention to the introduction. There is not much to do during the film or video and you want to impress on your audience that you are the presentation. The film or video is to support your presentation, not take it over.

Film, video monitors and projection television require special audio visual support. Even though you depend upon this support, you are still responsible for the total presentation. As with the projector, this means checking the equipment and coordinating with the audio visual personnel to ensure that proper preparations have been made.

Cut-Aways, Mock-Ups, and Props

Cut-aways, mock-ups and props can be effective for small presentations up to twenty-five people.

Anything you include that people can touch is usually going to increase retention. If you are talking about ABS pipe, show what the pipe looks like. If you are discussing meters and how they work, try to get a meter that has been cut away, revealing the inner diaphragm structure. How do car manufacturers advertise the strength of the steel guard beams in the sides of their cars? They show a cut-away of the car door that reveals the four-inch bars of steel that protect during a collision. Props are tangible objects that people can see. If they can see it, they will remember it.

Handouts

Distributing information about your presentation to the audience serves as a visual aid and helps build retention. Handouts should be clean and uncluttered reflecting the quality of your presentation.

The basic types of handouts are:

- Handouts that help an audience follow the presentation, such as outlines, diagrams, and models, *must be distributed immediately.*

- Task-oriented handouts on which members of the audience may do an exercise, take a test, play a game, etc., *are to be distributed immediately prior to using.*

- Handouts for continued learning, such as the actual text of the presentation, highlights, quotes, bibliographies, reprints, etc., *should be handed out immediately after the presentation is concluded.*

You may wish to advise your audience that handouts will be forthcoming at the end of the presentation. You want the attention of your listeners focused on you. Anything your listeners have in their hand or in front of their eyes competes for their attention.

Room Layout Guidelines

Where to hold your presentation and display your visuals can be a challenge because the ideal meeting room is hard to find. If it can handle 300 people, it will be too large for a group of 12. If it's an elaborately set-up room for a board of directors, it's not a good place for a department staff meeting. You must utilize the available facilities to optimize your presentation. To assist in room selection and set-up, the typical meeting room arrangements are illustrated (Figure 4.2). These arrangements contain recommended set-ups for location of lecterns, projectors, screens and seating for various size groups.

The final test for any room you are considering is to ask yourself these three questions:

1. Is it an appropriate size for this group?

2. Will it accommodate visual aids?

3. Does it have satisfactory acoustics, ventilation and access for participants?

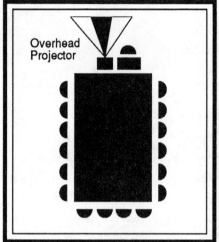

Center table arrangement. Suitable for under 20 people. This set-up promotes discussion and is best for long meetings.

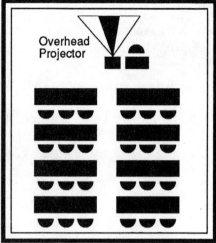

Classroom arrangement. This is a standard set-up for any size group.

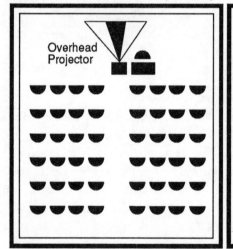

Auditorium/theater arrangement. Suitable for any size audience but most efficient for large groups.

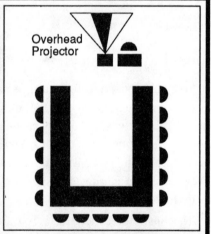

U-table arrangement. Suitable for 30 people or fewer. This arrangement is ideal for group discussion and interaction.

Figure 4.2   Room Layout

Chapter 5

Effective Delivery

How you deliver your presentation has greater impact on your audience than the actual words you speak. People do not carry away information from a speech, they carry away an impression, an impression that is built upon verbal and non-verbal communication.

Verbal and Non-Verbal Communication Channels

When making your delivery to an audience you use both verbal and non-verbal channels to communicate your message. To perform an effective delivery, you must become skilled at using both. The verbal channel (the words you speak) represents seven percent of the message. The non-verbal channel conveys how you look and sound. It carries the remaining ninety-three percent of your message to the audience. To better understand how these channels operate, it is useful to identify and contrast the properties of each. Some of these properties are:

Verbal Channel	Non-Verbal Channel
Words	Body language, Voice
Conscious	Unconscious
Descriptive of Emotion	Actual Emotion
Logical	Intuitive
Formal	Informal
Truth content can be manipulated	Truth content reliable

An important difference between these channels is in your conscious awareness of each. Since childhood, we have spent an enormous amount of time and energy mastering language. Conversely, non-verbal language has been enjoyed and has never been perceived as possibly belonging to an equally vast, organized communication system.

As a direct result of our education, we have gained a higher degree of control over our verbal output and can easily manipulate it. We are not as adept in controlling or altering the non-verbal messages and, as a result, the non-verbal channel accurately reflects our true underlying meanings. If we are out of touch with our real feelings or choose to conceal them, our verbal statements become descriptions of how we think we ought to feel, while our emotions, as revealed through our non-verbal cues, contradict our speech. It is important to understand that when feelings and verbal behavior coincide, the verbal and non-verbal signals transmitted are congruent. This is the climate best suited for optimum communication, but frequently verbal and non-verbal messages become mixed. The listener picks up this discrepancy and must select for himself the real intent of the message. The listener invariably relies on his non-verbal instincts and chooses to believe the non-verbal messages.

Utilizing Non-Verbal Messages

Non-verbal messages, if properly orchestrated, will enhance your delivery by enriching the presentation content. If you concentrate on sending positive messages, you will make a good impression by appearing more confident, animated and relaxed. Your facial expressions, eye contact, posture and physical gestures will coincide and support your presentation content. Here is a list of positive and negative messages:

	These Communicate Positive Messages	These Communicate Negative Messages
Facial	Smiling	Tight-lipped
	Relaxed mouth	Jaw muscles clenched
	Alert	Grim smile
	Ready to listen	Raised eyebrows
		Frown
Eyes	Pupils dilated	"Looking down nose"
	Good contact	Lack of contact
	Wide open	Narrowed

Head	Straight	Shaking back and forth
	Nodding up and down	Tilted
		Bowed
Body	Open	Crossed arms
Position	Erect	Legs crossed away
	Leaning forward	Cold shoulder
Hand	Open hands	Tapping fingers
Gesture	Steepling	Hiding mouth
	Hand to chest	Finger wagging
	Touching	Closed/clenched hand

Using your voice to send positive messages to your audience will also make you appear more confident, animated, relaxed and articulate. This is accomplished by the proper use of your voice attributes; pace, pauses, pitch and volume to support your delivery with the proper phrasing and emphasis. Professional speakers, actors and entertainers recognize the importance of the non-verbal channel and use it to improve their delivery and performance. You should learn from the professionals and follow their lead.

Delivery Problems

A moderate amount of fear can have a positive affect on a presentation by giving the speaker excitement and energy. However, excessive fear, causes nervousness which is displayed in the speaker's delivery through distracting mannerisms. The most common distractions that you should avoid are:

- Rigid body posture that inhibits natural gestures:

    Fig Leaf – stiff body with hands clasped tightly in front.
    Reverse Fig Leaf – stiff body with hands clasped tightly behind waist.
    Cling For Life – rigid body with hands tightly clasping the lectern.
    Ships Captain – stiff body leaning against the lectern.

- Swaying or rocking motion.

- Pacing.

- Thumping or tapping on the lectern or flip charts, etc.

- Staring at lectern notes or other objects such as the floor or ceiling.

Develop an Image That is You

The best way to relax and avoid delivery problems is to be yourself. Trouble begins when you try to become something you are not. The more deeply you accept yourself as you are, the more comfortable and relaxed you will be in making your delivery.

Each of us has a unique personality and delivery style. You should analyze your style and take full advantage of your strong points to project a positive image. Your weak points should be identified so that you can develop a personal strategy for change. Such a strategy may look like Figure 5.1

Personal Delivery Change Strategy			
	Image I Project	**Image I Would Like to Project**	**Personal Change Strategy**
My Visual Image	Too Casual	More Businesslike	Wear Better Quality Clothing
My Body: How Relaxed I Am; My Posture; How I Move	Inhibited in Movement, Gestures	More Relaxed, Easygoing	Practice Gesturing More Freely
My Non-Verbal Behavior	Not Enough Eye Contact	Warmer, More Involved With My Audience	Develop Better Eye Contact
My Spoken Image	Too Authoritative	More Sensitive	Audience Awareness
My Voice	Too High-Pitched	More Depth	Practice Voice Exercises

Figure 5.1   Personal Delivery Change Strategy

Manuscript Delivery

The impact and credibility of a person who reads a speech rarely approaches that of a speaker who delivers it from memory. If you are going to give a manuscript presentation, you should familiarize yourself with the ideas of the speech and then give it in your own words with your own personality. If you must read it word for word, then you should follow these guidelines:

- When your speech is written by someone else you should provide input.

- Impose your personality at the very beginning of the speech by using your own words and coming across as an individual .

- Deliver it with direct eye contact.

To deliver a manuscript speech well, you must be in control of your spoken image. You must be a good sight reader. In short, you must be a seasoned performer. If you are not, you are better off making an extemporaneous presentation.

Using Pointers for Emphasis

Pointers, when used correctly, can enhance delivery by drawing emphasis to your visual aids. Hold the pointer so you can point at your visual while facing the audience. If your visual aid is on your right as you face your audience, the pointer goes in your right hand; if on the left it goes in the left hand. If you have important things to say about your visual, you will make a greater impact if you face the audience as you speak. When you are through using the pointer, it is best to get it out of the audience's view. Set it down or if it is a telescoping pointer, collapse it and put it in your pocket. Keeping a pointer in your hand becomes a distraction.

Using Microphones for Volume

Microphones provide volume but will not put energy or excitement into your delivery. They allow you to reach out to the audience but will not put conviction into your voice. Fixed lectern microphones will restrict your movement and amplify any tapping or thumping sounds that you make. If possible, use a neck microphone called a lavaliere to avoid these problems.

Managing the Question and Answer Session

Managing questions is an important part of your presentation delivery because the audience continues to judge you through the question and answer session. The audience believes that answering questions requires spontaneity on your part and provides them the opportunity to see the real you in action.

If you plan to offer a question and answer session, always advise your audience in advance that there will be an opportunity to ask questions. When answering questions, be polite and follow these general guidelines:

- Listen to the question and give yourself time to think.

- Acknowledge the question and make sure you understand it.

- Make certain the question is answered satisfactorily.

- When possible answer more than yes or no.

- Do not answer a question with a question.

Answering Difficult Questions

Most questions are straightforward and have no hidden agendas. They can be answered simply and directly, but there are some kinds of questions that have pitfalls and which come up so frequently that you need to recognize them and know how to manage them:

The *Don't Know Question* - This is the kind of question you wish you could answer. Your best response is to be honest and reply: "I do not know, but I will find that information and get back to you." If the question is outside of your area of expertise, you should say exactly that.

The Loaded Question - A confrontational question that contains negative or highly confrontational language (price gouging, ripping-off the public, etc.). Your best response is to say very little. Never repeat the question using the same negative language. Your response could be: "I strongly disagree and would never use those words."

The Hypothetical Question - Some questions describe circumstances and invite you to speculate about their effect. You should not accept the premise of the hypothetical question and respectfully decline to speculate. If you do decide to respond to this type of question, make it absolutely clear that your answer is only speculation.

The Forced Choice - This question only offers you two alternatives for answers, and the problem is either answer may be wrong. Your best defense for this type of question is awareness. You should pause and your answer should refer to both, or neither answers, as being right or wrong.

The Multiquestion - Some questions become one lengthy run-on question. In this situation, you should simply pick out the one question you most want to answer and respond.

Managing Difficult Questioners

Questioners, as well as questions, can be tricky to handle. Listed below are a few types of questioners you should be aware of:

The Troublemaker - This is a person with a personal problem or an axe to grind. He makes a negative statement that usually is not a question at all. The best way to handle this individual is to offer to discuss the question in more detail after the presentation.

The Detailer - This person likes to quibble with facts and figures and draw you into a debate. If you respond with a long conversational answer you will lose your audience. If you are sure of the facts, stand by them. If you are not, you should discuss the issue after the presentation.

The Filibuster - This individual desires control and will launch into rambling and run-on statements. The most effective way to regain control without appearing rude is to look directly at the person and call him by name. This will cause him to pause, and then you can start talking.

Developing Effective Delivery Skills

Effective delivery skills are developed through practice. The first step is to become aware of what elements constitute a good presentation delivery. You build awareness by reading this book and watching accomplished speakers and television announcers. Once you understand the elements of good delivery, then you practice and perfect your technique. The objective of practice is to develop good delivery skills and habits; then that expertise is transferred to your subconscious by repetition. The result is giving a smooth presentation delivery without having to think about the mechanics. Your actions in front of the audience will be automatic and appear natural.

Listed below are basic guidelines that will help develop your delivery skills. You should follow these guidelines by practicing them in rehearsal and reviewing them prior to your presentation.

Delivery Guidelines

- Memorize your introduction and conclusion.

- Step up to the lectern with poise and authority.

- Pause and survey the audience before you begin speaking.

- Pick out friendly faces and smile as you begin to speak.

- Maintain good eye contact with the audience. If you need to look at your notes, stop talking, look down, then look up and resume.

- Keep your hands at waist level and allow yourself to gesture naturally. Avoid rigid body postures.

- Always face your audience. Never turn your back on your listeners.

- Speak important phrases slowly.

- Pause to let your listeners absorb information.

- Vary your pitch for emphasis.

- Keep phrases short so you can deliver them in one breath.

- Be yourself. Take full advantage of your own personality and project your unique delivery style.

- When you have finished, say so and step down.

Chapter 6

Personal Appearance

Your personal appearance is the first thing people see. It tells them how confident you are and how they should treat you. If you don't have enough self-respect to stand straight and dress properly, others may feel that you do not warrant respect from them.

Presentation Posture

Your posture is the key to communicating your image. A posture that is too stiff communicates uptightness, while a posture that is too loose communicates sloppiness and carelessness. A hunched over back and neck that is too far forward shows a lack of confidence and low self-esteem.

Developing good posture habits will improve your presentation image and the way you feel about yourself. Sitting erect instead of slumping can help you feel more important and help turn negative feelings about yourself into positive ones. In order to develop and keep good posture habits, you must properly condition your subconscious mind by consciously visualizing and practicing good posture habits.

One of the best techniques for examining your posture is to record yourself on videotape. You should first observe how you stand and how you sit. For good standing posture, stand up straight with your shoulders back and your stomach pulled in. To have good posture when sitting, it is important to sit all the way back in your chair. Your back will automatically become straight as it rests against the chair back.

Presentation Dress

Presentation dress is special, because it can add powerful support to your physical presence. A neat, business-like appearance will help immensely in getting your message across. Poorly chosen clothing that may be acceptable in the environment of your office may be distracting to an audience. Dress codes differ from industry to industry and profession to profession. You should be aware of these standards and dress accordingly.

Emphasize Quality

There is a lot that can be said about clothing styles; colors, patterns, and fabrics, but the single most important thing to remember is quality. A superior quality business suit communicates an image of confidence and status. The fact that you will feel more confident and influential is an important reason for wearing fine clothing. Your professional appearance will put you in a positive mood and add to your performance.

Clothing Guidelines

You should always plan your presentation objective first; then, with that objective firmly in mind, consider your presentation dress by following these guidelines:

Guidelines for Men

- Suits
    - Wear wool, tropical-weight for summer.
    - Dark colors are best, navy, charcoal and black. Gray is acceptable.
    - Pinstripes are acceptable in most industries, and required in some.
    - Vests are not recommended because they are too restrictive to breathing and movement.
    - Leave your jacket buttoned, unless seated.
- Shirts
    - Cotton or cotton blend fabrics are best.
    - A white shirt is recommended except when appearing before bright lights (television studio, video filming, etc.).
    - Solid colors are recommended, but pinstripes are acceptable.
    - Long sleeves with button-down or classic pointed collars are required.

- Ties

  - Silk is best with solid or simple pattern.

  - A conservative color is required.

- Jewelry

  - A watch and ring are fine.

  - Service pins are acceptable.

  - Avoid anything that calls attention to itself.

- Shoes

  - Conservative, black shoes are recommended.

  - Polished shoes in excellent condition are required.

- Hair

  - Clean haircut above the ear.

Guidelines for Women

- Suits

  - Suits are perfectly acceptable. Wool and silk are excellent choices; good cut and fit are important.

  - Hem line should be conservative. Knee-length is recommended as standard for presentation dress.

  - Wear conservative colors.

- Blouses

  - Cotton and silk are best.

  - Colors and patterns should be conservative.

  - Ruffled and laced fronts are acceptable if not overdone.

- Dresses

  - Wear cotton, wool or silk.

  - Colors and styles should be conservative.

  - Busy patterns and plunging necklines are not acceptable.

- Ties

    - Ties are optional.

    - Designer ties are nice and a silk scarf is a good alternative.

- Hose

    - Neutral to dark tones look best.

    - Conservative textures and patterns are acceptable but should not be overdone..

- Shoes

    - Wear closed end shoes with at least a little heel, conservative and matching your clothing.

    - Avoid boots, open toes and sling backs.

- Hair

    - Almost any length and style will work. Be conservative and avoid any excessive style.

    - Keep the hair pulled away from your face, especially your eyes.

    - If you use hair coloring, it should be conservative, match your complexion and not be obvious that it needs to be recolored.

- Jewelry

    - Pearls are great but leave your diamonds at home.

    - Keep it simple and avoid distracting dangling earrings and necklaces.

- Makeup

    - Makeup is usually a must but do not overdo.

    - Heavier makeup is required for video and film presentations.

    - Use conservative shades.

Final Advice

When you are making an important presentation or speech, make a point to wear something you like and makes you feel good. If your clothing makes you feel great, you will project a more confident and positive image.

Chapter 7

Your Vocal Image

If you react to speakers by the way they talk, you can be sure that your audience will be judging you the same way. They are making decisions about you and your message based upon their perception of your vocal image. Usually it is not what you say that creates this image, but how you say it.

Vocal Quality

A vocal image is what most of us associate with the term timbre. Timbre or vocal quality is the unique sound or characteristic of an individual's voice. It is determined by the resonating sound within the echo chambers of the chest, mouth, nose, cheekbones and head.

With the advent of audio and video recording equipment, people have become more self-confident about the way they sound. Some individuals feel frustrated and think nothing can be done to improve their voice, but you can change the way you sound, which can change how other people feel and act about you. If you do not have a naturally pleasant voice, consider devoting some time and effort to improving it by finding a voice teacher.

Vocal Inflection

There is more than timbre to consider about vocal quality. Learning how to effectively control and use the elements of voice inflection can have a dramatic effect on the way you phrase and emphasize your speech. Vocal inflection specifically refers to how your voice is varied. These variables include pace, pitch, volume, and pause.

Pace

Words spoken at a steady even pace take on a sameness and tend to blur together. Varying the pace of your words and phrases adds more meaning and stimulates interest.

The normal speaking pace is between 140 and 185 words per minute. The human brain can absorb information up to 800 words per minute, so your audience will be thinking about what you say. You should vary your pace to group words into meaningful clusters that give emphasis to key words and phrases. This means pushing together groups of relatively unimportant words and slowing down for the important key words that you want people to think about. In some cases, speaking faster can actually increase comprehension by tying thoughts together, but you must speak clearly to be understood.

Pitch

A monotonous, boring voice is the number one killer of vocal projection. So much of the meaning of what you really want to say is lost when you lack voice excitement. Clearly, the rise and fall of vocal pitch is a key element in effective speech. In most cases a low-pitched voice is considered an asset. For a man to sound credible and confident his voice needs to be lower in pitch. For a woman to be successful in business, she needs to use a lower pitched voice which will make her sound strong and assertive.

Volume

Always speaking at the same volume level can be drab and unexciting. You should speak loud enough to be heard by everyone, but vary the volume to add variety.

Pauses

Inexperienced speakers are afraid to pause while speaking, even for a moment. A three-second pause to these people seems like an eternity. They believe that during a pause no communication takes place. This is not true. Pauses are a vital element of non-verbal communication and are essential for a strong delivery. Pauses aid a presentation in the following ways:

- They carry a non-verbal message of their own by making the speaker appear relaxed, thoughtful and confident.

- They assist verbal comprehension by giving the audience time to absorb and think about a visual aid.

- They signal transitions by telling the audience that a thought element has been completed and, here comes the next point.

- When placed in the middle of a phrase or sentence they create emphasis by calling attention to what follows.

Phrasing and Emphasis - Verbal Punctuation

In verbal communication, we do not have the tools and convenience of punctuation to help bring out the meaning of our words. When we speak, we depend upon vocal inflection to create phrasing and emphasis.

A verbal phrase is an organized unit of thought, a group of words that expresses a single idea in one breath. Another way to think of a verbal phrase is, one thought equals one breath (one thought equals one phrase). This creates a *thought rhythm*. The speaker stops after each phrase, takes a breath and speaks the next phrase. For example, here is a sentence and how it might be phrased:

An attractive and effective speaking voice (breath) is based upon variety in tempo (breath) loudness (breath) pitch and timbre.

The natural lift that occurs after each phrase—as we pause to take a breath—signals the listener that we have completed one idea or thought element and are about to start another. People speak in shorter word groupings than they write, because it is easier for the audience to follow. The typical written sentence runs fifteen to twenty-three words; the average spoken sentence is eight to ten.

Emphasis is a powerful tool that gives you the opportunity to enhance the meaning of your words by directing the listeners' attention to what is important. Emphasis is also used as verbal punctuation to call attention to selected words or groups of words. In addition to pointing out key ideas, emphasis can add meaning to what we say. For example, by changing the emphasis of the following message, each reading will convey a slightly different message:

He will not go.	(stresses identity)
He *will* not go.	(suggests stubbornness)
He will *not* go.	(flat contradiction)
He will not *go*.	(defiant proclamation)

Emphasis can be used to enhance your presentation content by using any one of the following vocal inflection methods:

- **Changing pace** - Emphasizes key points by slowing down for certain phrases or thought groups. This is especially effective when combined with changes in pitch and volume.

- **Changing pitch** - Creates interest by emphasizing thought groups with an upward or downward change in pitch. Prevents speech from becoming monotonous.

- **Changing volume** - Creates emphasis by contrast. Both increasing volume and decreasing volume are effective.

- **Pauses** - Creates emphasis by providing anticipation or absorption time before or after a key word, phrase, thought or visual aid.

Fortunately, inflection is easy to improve on your own with practice and, once mastered, will improve your vocal image by making your speech more pleasant and easier to understand.

Diction and Pronunciation

The way you pronounce words can be a big factor in influencing people. People who mispronounce words usually are thought to be poorly educated or not very bright. This reputation can be completely unfounded because many mispronunciation problems are caused by bad diction habits, or past environmental factors. Most pronunciation and diction problems can be corrected by practicing good diction habits or receiving instruction from a qualified speech instructor.

Proper Grammar and Vocabulary

Inexperienced speakers are often intimidated by not having good grammar skills or an adequate vocabulary. This adds to their lack of self-confidence and results in poor speaking performance.

Using incorrect grammar can definitely keep you from getting ahead professionally, as well as socially. Most people perceive those who use correct grammar to be more intelligent and more successful than those who do not. Anyone can learn to use correct grammar by studying a high school English book.

You do not have to be a college graduate to have a good speaking vocabulary. You can build your vocabulary quickly by being on the lookout for new words and practice using them. For example, you can utilize the time spent going to and from work by investing in vocabulary tapes for your car cassette player. You can learn many new words over a period of twelve months.

Voice Problems

Voice is a problem when it calls attention to itself. Common voice problems are:

- Harshness - Unless physical in nature, this indicates tension and stress. These can be eliminated by using relaxing techniques and increasing your self-confidence.

- Nasality - Caused in most cases by not opening jaws wide enough when speaking. It can be eliminated by opening the mouth wider and using the tongue more firmly.

- Breathlessness - Weak and wavering voice caused by insufficient breathing when speaking. Can be corrected by taking deeper breaths and releasing a controlled flow of air.

- Filler Words - Distracting filler words like "ah," "oh," "um," or "and" are often substituted for a natural pause. To break the filler word habit, a speaker should take a breath for a second, hold it and then begin to speak.

Change Your Vocal Image

The goal of improving the way you sound is *not* to sound like everyone else, but to help develop your best-sounding image. The first thing to do is carefully look at, and listen to, yourself. You must objectively see and hear yourself speak, the way your audience perceives you. A video camera and recorder are great investments for evaluating and improving your vocal image. Not only can you observe yourself, but you can keep a record of your progress. At each practice session, increase your vocal variety by following these guidelines:

- Vary your pitch for emphasis.

- Speak important phrases slowly.

- Pause after an important phrase or key point.

- Occasionally speak in a quiet, confidential tone to make a point.

- Keep phrases short so you can deliver them in one breath.

- Practice feeling and expressing these basic emotions:

Happiness	Disgust
Anger	Love
Sadness	Sympathy
Surprise	Boredom
Fear	Doubt

Chapter 8

Surviving a Media Interview

Considering current telecommunications capabilities and the power of the press, being interviewed by news reporters can be a risky business. If a company spokesman says the wrong thing or is misunderstood, his statement can be heard in minutes by millions of people from coast to coast and can create severe consequences for his company. A speaker is at a disadvantage when talking to a reporter as they are skilled in asking provocative questions and are primarily interested in controversial answers. Even though the media does control the high ground, there are rules and guidelines a speaker can follow that will keep him out of trouble.

Media Interview Rules

The first interview rule is to have a sound, positive mental attitude. There is no room for an arrogant, uncaring or negative personality. You must project an image of competence, knowledge, warmth and respect. A negative attitude can, and probably will, be skillfully exploited by a reporter.

The second rule is to always be prepared for the media interview. The speaker should never walk into an interview planning to improvise. A successful interview is like giving a successful presentation. It requires careful and extensive preparation. The best way to prepare is to anticipate the most likely questions, research the facts, and prepare effective answers ready for use. It is important to remember the reporter is asking questions that viewers, readers, and listeners want answered.

Media Interview Guidelines

Now that you understand the interview ground rules, here are the guidelines for you to follow:

Most Important Facts First

State the most important facts first. People tend to remember more clearly the first and last things that are said. It is best to give the reporter your conclusion first, because the end of your interview may be cut off and omitted for technical reasons. A newspaper reporter seldom knows in advance how much space will be available for his story. He has been trained to put the most important facts first, using subsequent paragraphs to report items of lesser interest. On television, time pressure and broadcast deadlines often make it impossible to screen all filmed footage for selection of the best material. This often forces program producers or news editors to select segments from the beginning of a film or video tape and omit a segment at the end.

Viewpoint of the Public

Speak from the viewpoint of the public's interest, not your company's. You must step back and look at your company's position and your statement from the public's point of view. The public knows, or believes, that a company primarily acts in its own self-interest. When this self-interest is not frankly admitted, credibility is lost.

Personal Terms

Talk in personal terms whenever possible. The words "the company" or "we" only reinforce the public impression of corporations as impersonal monoliths in which no one retains his individuality or has any individual responsibility. If you speak in terms of your personal experience, you will always make a favorable impression.

Lying and Concealment

Tell the truth. In this era of extreme competition, hostility and corruption, it seems that the most difficult task of all is simply telling the truth. Understandably, nobody likes to admit mistakes or report bad news; yet telling the truth remains the best policy. Intelligent people understand that the uncertainties in our world and the difficulties of management make errors in judgement unavoidable. What the public will not understand or tolerate is dishonesty. Concealment and lying will not be forgotten nor forgiven by the public or the media.

Off the Record Statements

If you do not want a statement quoted, do not make it. You should avoid all "off-the record" statements because there is really no such thing. The statement may well turn up in a published article, minus your name, and with a qualifying phrase added, "it has been learned from other sources . . ." The damage is done.

If you do not want something used or published, don't divulge it to the reporter. Simply say, "I cannot comment on that at this time," and state the reason. The reporter will understand.

Losing Your Temper

Don't argue with a reporter or lose your temper. You cannot win the argument as the reporter is in control of the published or televised story lines. If a reporter interrupts you, it is not out of rudeness; it is a deliberate technique that means he is not satisfied with the response he is hearing. The solution is to respond more directly and more clearly. You must give the reporter full cooperation; if you don't, the battle may be won but he will win the war. The reporter, not you, will write the story.

Reporter's Tricks

If a question contains offensive language or words that are inappropriate to your statement, do not repeat them, even if it is to deny them. Reporters often use the techniques of putting words into your mouth. For example, "Mr. James, are your company's excess profits this year due to the fact that you have a monopoly on the market?" If Mr. James takes the bait, he may answer, "No, our company profits are not due to a monopoly." Mr. James' answer can then be headlined, "Profits not due to monopoly." Even though Mr. James denied the charge, in the public's mind, he has associated the words "company profits" with "monopoly." Be aware and do not fall for this trick. The reporter knows that his questions will not be quoted in his article; only your answers will appear.

Clarifying the Questions

Listen carefully to the question, and take time to think before you answer. Reporters have a tendency to fire questions in rapid succession. You must not let yourself be rushed into giving answers. You should listen carefully to each question being asked.

If it is not clear or if you believe there is a hidden meaning, make the reporter clarify the question. After all, you are the one that will be quoted, not the reporter.

The "Public Interest"

The most important point to remember during media interviewing is that the reporter's first responsibility is to produce a newsworthy story that will satisfy the "public interest." The reporter does not care if that story will help or hinder your company. The reporter will use whatever techniques are required to accomplish his or her goal. It is your responsibility as a speaker to remember this. When the time comes to meet the media, be prepared!

Chapter 9

Speaking On Camera

Satellite communication capabilities and video teleconferencing are growing rapidly. With more companies utilizing all aspects of television and video communications, the likelihood that you will find yourself speaking on camera is increasing. When that day arrives, every element of your dress, grooming, posture, gestures and speech will be under close scrutiny for everyone to see. If you do not perform in a competent and credible manner, your career could be in trouble.

The simplest way to avoid a "first appearance on camera" fiasco is to be prepared. No one ever walks up to a live camera and does well without preparation and experience. Most people who are relaxed and perform well in regular meetings and presentations become nervous upon their first exposure to a film or video interview. The reason video appears so intimidating is the impersonal way the camera looks at you without a live audience. To perform well on camera (as with anything else in life that you want to do well), you must practice.

On Camera Training

You can learn how to perform through professional training. Most major cities have communications consultants who conduct training workshops on public speaking, sales training and media interviews. These professionals reinforce your strengths while eliminating any distracting mannerisms. The training sessions provide valuable experience in a semi-studio environment with up-to-date equipment. Some consultants provide teleprompter training for manuscript presentations and television announcing.

Rehearsing On Camera

If a professional on-camera consultant is not available, you can rehearse by using a company or home video camera, recorder, and lights.

To be successful in the video media, you must rehearse until your performance becomes second nature. In order to project a favorable image on camera, you must think on your feet, anticipate where the interviewer is trying to lead you and avoid dangerous issues. You do not have time to be self-conscious. You must be free to concentrate on the content of the interview and not on your non-verbal performance.

As you rehearse, you will begin to understand that television is more intimate visually and orally than a speech to a live audience. The television audience will be able to see you at extremely close-up range, and you will not have to project your voice any more than you would in a normal conversation. Body movement and facial expressions are magnified on television, so it is important to be relaxed and make smooth gestures.

If you are practicing for a media interview, have someone drill you with questions, critique your on-camera performance, and review your verbal and non-verbal messages.

At first, you will feel awkward and intimidated, rehearsing in front of a camera and lights. The experience will seem artificial. You must develop your self-confidence through practice, through positive self-talk and the visualization techniques discussed earlier. As your confidence increases, your voice and gestures will become more natural and relaxed. You will begin to see yourself from a new perspective, and like what you see. However, to build your on-camera confidence, you must be willing to do the work and rehearse. Here are some guidelines that will help:

Video Rehearsal Guidelines

- The camera records all of your verbal and non-verbal signals. You must always be yourself and tell the truth. "The camera doesn't lie."

- Likability on television is more important than anything else. Be relaxed and smile.

- Television magnifies movement. Don't make any fast moves, you'll go right off camera. Use less body energy and slow down your eye and head movements on close-ups. Whatever is closer to the camera appears bigger.

- Sudden moves toward or away from the camera are likely to get you out of focus.

- Get your lungs full of air before you speak; it adds projection to your voice and helps prevent voice problems.

- A five o'clock shadow looks terrible on television. The lights make it look worse than it is. Men must shave closely.

- Dress conservatively in solid colors. Stripes and checks are busy and bleed on the television screen. Avoid large blocks of white. White creates what is called white noise on television.

Using the Teleprompter

If you are planning to deliver a manuscript presentation or present an exact statement on television or videotape, you will be using a teleprompter.

The teleprompter is an electronic video system that enables you to read text while appearing to look directly into the camera. There are two common types: one is a video monitor located just below the camera lens, the other is a glass sheet or screen usually placed over the camera lens. Both types display about six lines of text and are easy to read.

Because you are reading text and generally have no audience present, it is difficult to relax and give a smooth delivery. Being a good sight reader is a big help, but practice is the key to giving a professional performance. Finding a teleprompter on which to practice is not easy. It requires a trained operator and is expensive equipment to rent. Your best bet is to either request rehearsal time at the studio or retain the services of a professional communications consultant.

When you rehearse with the teleprompter, it is important to lead the text, do not follow! The teleprompter operator will vary the speed of the text display based upon your lead. As you read the text, remember to smile, gesture, and pause.

The Television Studio

Once you have thoroughly rehearsed for your on camera appearance, you are ready to meet the television studio.

A television studio is a beehive of activity. Technicians, cameramen and stagehands are busy giving hand signals, rearranging sets and props while various visitors walk through. This totally new environment will unnerve you at first, but once you familiarize yourself with studio operations your apprehension will subside. If you are scheduled for an on camera appearance, a guided study tour should be arranged. If a tour is not possible, do whatever is necessary to get a behind-the-scenes look, even if it means locating programs that welcome live audiences.

The Television Appearance

As soon as you enter the television studio, consider yourself on camera. It is not always clear when the camera is on, or which camera is being used. The studio director will signal the host and he will take the lead. There are numerous signals being passed around but don't be distracted. Concentrate on how you will use your time on camera. If you are not already seated when you are introduced, you must make an on camera entrance. It is good to project a smooth, confident image by walking on the set at an even pace, not too eager or too timid, and sit comfortably and securely facing your host. Do not look at the floor. You should be looking at your host or the audience, if there is one. Do not forget to smile. Remember that the audience will be seeing everything only from the point of view of the camera lens. If multiple cameras are used, the one with the red light glowing represents the audience. When you are speaking in a close-up, avoid licking or biting your lips or placing objects like a pen or pencil close to your face.

If a lavaliere (microphone) has been pinned to your clothing or placed around your neck, don't bump or rub it as you talk.

When you are asked a difficult or penetrating question, do not look up or down as though looking for a place to hide. If you must look away from the camera or the host in order to gather your thoughts, gaze behind the camera lens or past the interviewer. This will appear to the television viewers that you are facing a live audience in the studio and giving them your complete attention.

Do not be fearful of telling your host that you cannot answer a given question, but do include the reason why. When you think you have said enough and do not wish to offer any more information, just smile and stop talking. If you stay still, your host or studio crew will take the lead and cut away from you to something else. television is fast paced and all studio personnel are trained to avoid dead time.

Chapter 10

Speaking at Special Occasions

Impromptu Situations and Business Meetings

People in management positions or active in their communities are often called upon to speak at special occasions. These speaking opportunities provide speakers with excellent visibility and access to influential people. By using carefully chosen words in a public setting you can help people recognize the special occasion more clearly and vividly, while simultaneously projecting a positive image that adds to your status. The key to your success in this speaking area is to understand the different requirements of each occasion and be prepared.

Special Occasion Speeches

Most special occasion speeches fall into two general categories, those honoring individuals and those commemorating occasions. Examples of speeches honoring individuals are:

- Presentation and acceptance of awards.

- Welcomes and farewells.

- Inaugurations.

- Introductions.

- Eulogies.

Speeches commemorating occasions include:

- Keynote addresses.

- Commencement speeches.

- Dedications.

- Public relations (good will) speeches.

Vivid Language

All special occasion speeches involve the recognition of values that are important to society. The goal of these speeches is to be inspirational rather than informational or persuasive. The most important speaking skills for achieving this goal are choosing the right words to say and being sincere.

Vivid language will help express your thoughts about the occasion. Your choice of words should arouse emotion and focus the audience's thoughts and feelings on whom or what is being honored or commemorated. The key point of the speech must be committed to memory. A speech that is read is usually perceived as less sincere, unless you are an excellent sight reader and maintain good eye contact with the audience. The skills of speech organization and originality are less important in special occasion speeches because there are clear expectations of what your speech should contain. You must choose the appropriate language that will most vividly inspire recommitment to the values that the special occasion represents.

Honoring an Individual - The Introduction of a Speaker

The most common speech honoring an individual is the introduction of the speaker. Your two major goals in this type of speech are to establish the credibility of the guest speaker and increase interest for the speech. As an introducer, you need to consider those aspects of credibility that are important and expected on this occasion. Do not overpraise as this could embarrass and set up a standard that would be difficult for the speaker to meet. Speeches of introduction are usually brief and last from thirty seconds to two minutes, depending on the audience's familiarity with the speaker and how long he or she will be speaking. The introduction is directed toward the audience's interest, and it is helpful to check with the speaker about which things should be previewed and highlighted.

The Inauguration Speech

The inauguration speech is given by a person who is assuming the head of an organization or government. Inauguration speeches can include those delivered by the incoming president of a service club, such as Rotary, or the League of Women Voters. The objectives in this speech are to reaffirm the values of the organization you are about to head and to state the goals you will attempt to achieve while in that position. Here are the guidelines for you to follow:

- Note the achievements of your predecessor.

- Highlight your values and accomplishments.

- Indicate the new direction you and your administration will take.

The Welcoming Speech

There are many opportunities to welcome people into companies, professional associations, service clubs and other types of organizations. As a speaker, you are welcoming the person into new professional responsibilities and new personal relationships. The focus and expectation in the welcome speech is to associate the values of the welcoming group with those values possessed by the person being welcomed. State the benefits that will be the result of the new person joining the organization.

Presenting an Award

The organization or group presenting the award highlights the values the award represents. As the presentation speaker, you should cover the following points:

- The source or origin of the award.

- The nature of the award and the reasons for presenting it.

- The special merits of the person receiving it.

Emphasize the tribute, admiration and praise expressed for the recipient, rather than the award itself or its value.

Acceptance Speeches

When accepting an award, express your appreciation while minimizing your own accomplishments or merits. You may even modestly disclaim your own merits and give special recognition to your colleagues or others who have helped bring the honor to you. Give tribute to the donor of the award if it is appropriate. Adapt your response to the remarks of the donor and to the mood of the occasion. Your total acceptance response should be genuinely sincere and quite brief, unless you are a featured speaker.

The Farewell and Appreciation Speech

Farewell speeches are common today in our mobile society with young professionals often changing jobs and locations. This type of speech is also given at retirement ceremonies conducted by business, political and educational organizations. If you are speaking to honor someone who is leaving, pay tribute to the individual by recognizing the contribution the person has made and wishing him well in his future endeavor.

If asked to comment on your leaving, mention some of the outstanding experiences you shared with the people there and indicate how these experiences have contributed to your growth and enjoyment.

Speeches to Commemorate Occasions

The Dedication Speech

The dedication speech usually marks the completion of a new creation or the beginning of a major endeavor. The dedication speech should stress the spirit and meaning that the creation or endeavor represents. You should state the values of the creation or endeavor and inspire the audience to identify with these values. Examples of the dedication speech are dedicating a new building, work of art, or a speech to begin a fund-raising program.

The Keynote Address

Large organizations often begin their meetings with a keynote address which reflects the values of the association and provides a common orientation for the convention. The keynote speaker is usually an outstanding member of the organization or an individual who has high credibility with the audience. The speaker should highlight the goals of the organization and stress the importance of the convention, inspiring the audience's active participation.

The Public Relations Speech

The public relations speech is an important means of maintaining positive contact with the public. It is used in coordination with the efforts of an organization's public relations department in communicating a positive image. The speech is primarily persuasive in nature and is focused on promoting an image or idea rather than selling a specific product or service. The speaker should highlight the organization's mission and tie the company's goals to the values of the audience, indicating how the organization can benefit the audience. Keep in mind that friendliness, integrity and sincerity are essential for a good public relations speech.

Impromptu Situations

The Impromptu Talk

The impromptu talk is the one delivered without preparation. Inexperienced speakers sometimes make the mistake of attempting this type of delivery. They believe they will talk better if they leave everything to the inspiration of the moment. The problem is that the moment for speaking inevitably arrives but the inspiration seldom does.

Only the most accomplished speakers can handle the impromptu talk successfully. They have made so many prepared speeches they can readily draw upon this store of experience to make some apt remarks. Unless you are a pro, you should prepare your talk beforehand.

PREP Formula

If you cannot prepare your talk ahead of time and circumstances dictate that you suddenly rise and say a few words, you can still be prepared by knowing and following the PREP Formula. The formula consists of the following format:

P = Point
R = Reason
E = Example
P = Point

To use the PREP Formula, you simply follow this procedure:

- As quickly as possible, select a simple message or point; then state the point.

- Say it in another way, or give a reason for your point.

- Tell a story, or give an example to illustrate your point.

- Re-state your point in still another way, trying to say it even more strongly than before.

By following the PREP formula you can say your few words in an organized manner and because you are organized, you will do well.

Business Meetings

Conducting the Business Meeting

A well-organized and smoothly conducted business meeting can produce positive action and results. Being an effective chairman can help your career by demonstrating to people that you are organized and can get things done. Your objectives as chairman are: be a team player and inspire others to be responsible, take action and produce results. You can achieve these objectives by following the business meeting guidelines listed below.

Business Meeting Guidelines

- Prepare for the meeting by completing an agenda. Distribute it to all participants.

- Reconfirm before the meeting that the participant list and facilities are in order.

- Be organized and check to see that all meeting arrangements have been made such as name tags, visual aids, refreshments, etc.

- Begin with a good opening statement that includes a word of welcome, a review of the agenda, a statement of the ground rules and the expected closing time.

- Make the appropriate introductions if the members do not know each other.

- High priority items should be presented first. Only reports and results should be discussed at the meeting. Preparatory work should be done beforehand so that valuable time is not wasted.

- All potential outside interruptions should be eliminated.

- Make a decision as to the best format for the group (formal or informal), and stick with it. Motions and seconds pace and focus a meeting, but are inappropriate for an informal group.

- Make sure all issues are discussed fairly and all parties have equal opportunity to be heard.

- Summarize and gain consensus on what action items are needed, which individuals are responsible, and completion dates.

- Conclude the meeting on time.

- After the meeting, promptly prepare and distribute the meeting minutes to those attending and other appropriate parties.

Conference Centers

Many companies and organizations hold meetings and special occasion ceremonies at conference centers which offer excellent facilities. These centers are operated by professionals who offer many services including planning assistance.

You must however be cautious, while conference centers provide quality service, you are responsible as chairman or host to ensure that all arrangements have been made and the event runs smoothly. If you are not in charge, but you are speaking at the occasion, check out the facilities and meeting room beforehand and become familiar with the equipment.

Chapter 11

Presentations That Sell

In our free enterprise system, the sales function plays a vital role in keeping the doors of business open. The ability to sell is dependent upon several factors, but the one in which we are most interested, as a speaker or presenter is the sales presentation. The sales presentation requires the same careful planning, organization and delivery as other kinds of presentations but differs in that it utilizes persuasion to increase its effectiveness. To better prepare yourself as a speaker and presenter, you must understand what persuasion is and how it is used. Once you understand the basic process, you will be able to apply the principles of persuasion to your own speeches and sales presentations.

What Is Persuasion?

People make their own decisions, but many factors influence those decisions. When you persuade, you provide people with reasons for changing their minds or taking action on things they already believe. Persuasion is *not* using coercion to influence others, it *is* a legitimate attempt to make the best case you can, directing your appeals to your listeners' reason and emotions and basing them on your credibility as a speaker.

How Persuasion Works

It is human nature that people desire psychological balance and consistency in their life. This stability is maintained through one's knowledge, opinion or belief about the environment, about one's self, or about one's behavior. If a person encounters contradictory knowledge, opinions or beliefs, his or her psychological system is thrown out of balance. Psychologists refer to this experience as cognitive dissonance. The person tries to resolve the conflict and get back inside his or her comfort zone. In persuasion you attempt to influence the person to resolve the conflict as you would like it resolved. In other words, you provide an option you want acted upon, and if acted upon will put the other person at ease.

Influencing people to act can be difficult, especially when the action proposed involves discomfort, or physical or psychological danger. To cite an example, if you ask disgruntled employees to sign a petition to improve eating conditions in the company cafeteria, you could create conflicts within those who are afraid to identify themselves. They might resolve their internal conflict by rejecting your request, unless you convince them that the benefits in taking action outweigh the dangers. As a persuader, you must first encourage or generate the out-of-balance condition (cognitive dissonance) in your listeners' mind by increasing the conflict they already feel. Then you must offer a solution to the conflict that will restore balance by showing that something can be done. They can sign the petition and change the eating conditions.

You should use persuasion in presentations where people wish to resolve conflicts in their attitudes and beliefs. Your listeners will change their attitudes and beliefs by reacting to:

- Your appeal to their reason.

- Your appeal to their emotions.

- Your credibility as a speaker–your projected image as a sincere, trustworthy, believable person.

Persuasion cannot occur when you challenge your listeners' beliefs arrogantly and tactlessly. Your most effective use of persuasion will occur when you speak on a subject which you know thoroughly and which evokes strong, positive emotions in you.

Audience Needs as Factors in Persuasion

Salespeople have been telling us for years that in sales you do not sell *things*, you sell *emotions*. "You sell the sizzle not the steak."

When salespeople plan their sales presentation, they plan to satisfy needs. They have learned from experience that business buyers have three needs to fill:

1. The needs of the job function - equipment, material or other requirements to perform the job.

2. The needs of the company or organization - any item pertaining to achieving company goals and objectives, such as increasing sales and reducing costs.

3. Personal needs - those things that satisfy self-growth, recognition, promotion and security.

Marketing and salespeople tell us that these needs are interconnected, but when it comes to buying decisions people favor their personal needs. Studies indicate that people make decisions based on their personal perception of the situation, driven by emotion. Then they use logic and reasoning to justify the decision they have already made. Few of us will admit or even recognize our real motivations. Instead, we may adopt any of the following methods of justifying our actions:

- We seek evidence to justify, and reasons to explain what we have already said or done.

- We ignore evidence that contradicts what we have said or done.

- We reject the source of contradictory evidence.

The emotional and rational aspects of an audience are inextricably interwoven, and it is an illusion to believe otherwise. Your success in being persuasive is directly related to your ability to relate to the emotional needs of your audience.

Audience Beliefs as Factors in Persuasion

Persuasion can change your audience's beliefs, but there are limits. Your odds for succeeding decrease when you try to change your listener's firmly held beliefs.

The psychologist Milton Rokeach has devised a simple framework that helps classify the strength of beliefs. He divides them into three categories:

1. Peripheral Beliefs - Beliefs held least firmly and changed most frequently. These beliefs will be sacrificed when they conflict with stronger beliefs. An example would be giving up a belief to economize and buying a new sports car to have fun.

2. Authority Beliefs - Beliefs valued because of a person or situation from which they have originated. An example would be a change in diet on the advice of a doctor. The changing of authority beliefs is dependent upon the strength of conflicting beliefs of the person considered to be an authority.

3.   Core Beliefs - Beliefs that are central to personality and being. It would
be the same as losing an eye or one's life to give up these beliefs. They
are an ingrained part of what makes a person an individual and they
will not be relinquished under most circumstances. An example would
be giving up loyalty to one's country.

How your audience holds and relates to these three sets of beliefs determines the
effectiveness of your persuasive appeal. You can question their *peripheral beliefs*, and
maybe their *authority beliefs* by offering stronger conflicting knowledge, but stay away
from suggesting changes to their *core beliefs*. The core beliefs are used to stimulate action
only when your presentation agrees with these beliefs.

Using Emotional Appeals

One important fact to remember when dealing with an audience's emotions is that nobody
likes to be wrong. People will defend themselves emotionally if they are attacked or
cornered psychologically. Your strategy should be to explain to your listeners that they
are not wrong, their *information* is wrong. You must tell them that they are "okay" so
they will act "okay."

Emotional appeals should be used sensitively, skillfully, and sparingly, to support
and balance appeals to reason and logic. Excessive use of emotion in persuasion will only
insult your audience's intelligence and cause them to turn against you.

Appealing to Reason

To be truly convincing and to ensure that your presentation will sell, your arguments
must be logical and well-grounded in evidence. Evidence can take several forms, but to
be useful it must support your ideas and establish your point. Some examples of
supporting evidence are:

- Statistics and Facts.

- Personal experiences.

- Logical arguments supported by facts.

When planning your persuasive presentation, you must always consider the degree
of your listener's sophistication. Your audience's background, experience and intelligence will determine the proportion of the emotional and rational mixture. The intelligent,
well-educated audiences will be more responsive to an appeal to reason, based upon

evidence. They are more likely to respect a speaker who seems objective, and projects an image of being a person of reason.

Now that you understand the basics of persuasion, let's look at how to construct a presentation that sells.

Structuring the Sales Presentation

Once you have stated your sales presentation objective, thoughtfully considered your listeners' needs, attitudes and beliefs, and calculated how you will use your emotional and rational appeals, you are ready to establish your presentation structure. To ensure success, you should follow this persuasive four-step sales presentation strategy:

Step 1: Establish Your Credibility - First, establish rapport with your audience by projecting a trustworthy, likeable and believable image. This is done by being as confident as you are knowledgeable. You can state your credentials, experience and professional title, but to succeed you must be thoroughly in command of yourself and your materials.

Step 2: Define the Problem - Demonstrate that the problem really exists. Your audience may accept your contention that a problem exists; however, they may not agree on your interpretation of the causes. You should be prepared to concede and demonstrate that your audience's interpretation partially explains the problem, but does not satisfactorily explain the whole problem. Being able to predict and understand your audience's attitudes and beliefs about the real nature of the problem is crucial in this step.

Step 3: State the Solution - Explain your solution to the problem, comparing it to others. Next you should demonstrate and refute anticipated objections. Knowing that problems can have many solutions, you should address the solutions advanced by others and acknowledge their partial validity, yet stressing their errors. Then again state your solution to the problem while refuting objections.

Step 4: Moving Your Audience to Action - Picture and demonstrate how your audience will benefit from acting on your proposal. Induce your audience to act on your idea by proving that the solution is workable. You achieve this by demonstrating that your proposal is reasonable, practical, positively beneficial and non-threatening.

This four-step strategy offers a good workable framework for producing effective results. In certain circumstances, one or more of the steps may prove unnecessary and may be omitted. In other cases, the steps may need to be expanded or modified to meet requirements for special situations.

To help plan your presentation strategy, a sales presentation planning sheet is provided in Figure 11.1.

PERSUASIVE SALES PRESENTATION PLAN

PRESENTATION OBJECTIVES

DESIRED RESULTS: _____

FOUR-STEP STRATEGY

STEP 1: ESTABLISH CREDIBILITY

OPENING REMARKS: _____
CREDENTIALS: _____
AFFILIATIONS: _____
EXPERIENCE: _____

STEP 2: PROBLEM DEFINITION

AUDIENCE SOLUTIONS: _____
CONCESSIONS: _____
EMOTIONAL APPEALS: _____
EVIDENCE REQUIREMENTS: _____

STEP 3: PROBLEM SOLUTION

PROPOSED SOLUTION: _____
SOLUTIONS TO BE REFUTED: _____
EMOTIONAL APPEALS: _____
RATIONAL APPEALS: _____

STEP 4: CALL FOR ACTION *(CLOSE THE SALE)*

WORKABLE SOLUTION: _____
AUDIENCE BENEFITS: _____
LOW RISKS: _____
ACTION STATEMENT: _____

AUDIENCE PROFILE

AUDIENCE DEMOGRAPHICS

AGE: _____ ETHNIC IDENTITY: _____ SEX: _____
EDUCATION _____ INCOME LEVEL: _____
OCCUPATION OR
PROFESSIONAL STATUS: _____
POLITICAL AFFILIATION: _____

AUDIENCE APPEALS

EMOTIONAL: _____
RATIONAL: _____

AUDIENCE NEEDS

JOB FUNCTIONS: _____
COMPANY/ORGANIZATION: _____
PERSONAL: _____

AUDIENCE BELIEFS

PERIPHERAL: _____
AUTHORITY: _____
CORE: _____

Figure 11.1 Persuasive Sales Presentation Plan

Chapter 12

Personal Training Program

No book on public speaking can substitute for a valuable speaking experience. This section contains a thirty-day Personal Training Program designed to give this experience. The program is comprised of four speaking assignments that are to be given to a live audience such as a Toastmaster Club or company-sponsored speaking program.

If an audience is not available or if you prefer to train on your own, these assignments can be practiced and performed on camera with video equipment. Working with video provides the advantage of instant replay of your performance and helps identify and develop your own speaking style. If you choose to work alone, it is helpful to have a friend or supporter critique your performance.

The ideal training environment is performing before a live audience and recording the session on videotape. This gives the dual advantages of learning to be at ease before a group and seeing your performance on video.

Whichever method of training you choose, each speaking assignment will provide the opportunity to apply and practice the principles presented in this book. Don't worry about mistakes as you practice and perform each assignment. You will learn from each experience. During each training session, you will know that there is improvement because you will feel your self-esteem growing. Concentrate on completing each assignment one step at a time, and practice the delivery until it is right. If these suggestions are followed, you will be thrilled at the progress.

Assignment (Week-1)

The Ice Breaker

Presentation Objectives

Learn to be at ease before an audience or camera.

Identify your speaking style.

Identify the weak areas in your speaking skills which need to be strengthened.

Time

Two to three minutes

Your Assignment

The general subject of this talk is *you*. Select two or three interesting aspects of your life that will give insight and understanding of you as an individual, such as your birthplace, education, family, etc. Explain how you came to be in your present occupation and tell the audience something about your aspirations.

If you prefer to avoid an autobiography, you might talk about your business, your hobbies, or anything that relates to you as an individual. Having complete knowledge about your subject will add greatly to your confidence.

Weave the main points of your talk into a story, just as if you were telling it to friends.

Creating Your Talk

Your talk needs a beginning, a middle, and an ending. Try to create an interesting opening statement. Get the sentence clearly fixed in your mind, and use it even if a better idea occurs to you just before you speak. Then devise a good way to conclude, and fix that in your mind. With a good start and a good finish, you can easily fill in the body of the speech.

Select three or four main points and expand on them by use of examples, stories and anecdotes. Make a point, say it again in different words, illustrate the point, and then state it once more to be clearly understood. The audience will miss the point if you merely state a fact and continue on to the next fact of the subject. This is a good skill to learn with your first talk.

If you plan to use notes, write a brief speech outline on 3 x 5 cards which you can place on the lectern. Refer to them only when necessary. Remember, you are speaking, not reading. Many speakers write the entire speech, then break it down into parts with a key word for each part, and finally write just the key words on the cards.

Preparing Yourself

Now the talk is ready, but are you? You will need to rehearse. Practice the talk until you are comfortable with it. You will not need to memorize the talk since you are thoroughly familiar with the subject. Rather than thinking of this presentation as making a speech, think of it as a talk before a group of friends, sharing information of interest to them. Do not picture yourself as being afraid of the audience.

Presenting Your Talk

Once you have prepared your speech, relax. Feeling nervous is natural for all speakers regardless of the experience they have had. Put your nervous energy to work by using it to add excitement to the delivery of your talk. No one will pay attention to a quavering in your voice. The quavering will disappear as you become involved with your story.

Before you start to speak, take a few deep breaths and slowly exhale. Pause to let the audience settle down, then plunge in with your prepared opening statement.

While you are speaking, make eye contact with various members of the audience, first looking directly at one person for a few seconds, then looking at another, so no one feels left out of your talk. If you are speaking on camera, look directly into the camera lens as though you are talking to one individual. Be aware of and observe the time limit for your presentation.

Do not end your talk with a "Thank you." It is the audience who should thank you. Just give the audience your prepared closing statement and step down.

Assignment (Week-2)

Be Organized

Presentation Objectives

Organize your ideas into a logical sequence which leads the audience to a clearly defined goal.

Build a speech outline that includes an opening, a body and a conclusion.

Time

Five minutes

Your Assignment

In the previous assignment you had experience speaking before an audience or on camera. Now you are ready to concentrate on the structure of an effective speech. You must learn to organize your ideas and follow an outline from beginning to end.

Organization

Organization is clear thinking. Your speech must be organized in a logical and orderly manner so that it makes sense to your audience.

Always speak from your listener's point of view. Your listeners will be motivated by their interests, needs and beliefs. As you organize the talk, think of something to motivate agreement with you, understand you, or take action on your behalf, then develop your ideas to best support that motivation. Good organization and preparation are the keys to success.

Creating Your Talk

The first step in creating a talk is to decide what to talk about. Select a subject of interest to you and your audience, and then limit yourself to a single aspect of the subject. You will be speaking for only a few minutes, and will need all of that time to fully develop a single fact of the larger subject. Be sure that the topic is timely and relevant to your audience and one about which you can speak with some degree of authority, enthusiasm and conviction. Fix in your mind exactly what your purpose is in giving this talk. What specific point do you want to impress on your audience? Do you intend to explain, persuade, entertain or inspire? This decision will determine what your speech title will be, and how you will open and close the talk.

Select your ideas and arrange them into a logical sequence that leads to a conclusion. To achieve your speech goal, you should build on an outline.

Preparing Your Talk

You have several organization styles or outlines to choose from. Here is a sample outline sequence you can use that works well in business or training sessions:

1. Open with an exciting and challenging statement .

2. Give an illustration that brings the audience into the subject. You might begin, "Suppose you had an experience like this . . ."

3. Use an actual incident to emphasize the illustration: "As I drove onto the freeway, the engine quit."

4. Show a comparison or analogy to further clarify the point you are making.

5. Touch briefly on arguments that oppose your viewpoint, showing their errors.

6. Quote an authority, or use simple statistics to support your argument.

7. Close on a note similar to your opening and motivate your audience to action, agreement or understanding. The important point here is to bring your speech together into an integrated message.

Give special attention to your opening and closing statements. When you have created an effective opening and closing, memorize them, especially your first sentence. This will establish rapport with the audience and give clear starting and ending points around which to build. At this stage in your development, it is best to stick with a planned opening. Last minute changes will only confuse what should be a carefully laid out plan.

Presenting Your Talk

When you present your talk, the three most important things to remember are:

1. Good delivery or performance can enhance content. Poor delivery or performance can undermine content.

2. An audience carries away an impression of you that can outweigh the content of what you say.

3. How you look and sound constitutes ninety-three percent of the impression you make.

It is natural to be nervous. Some natural anxiety helps because it gives you energy. Keep calm, take a deep breath, visualize your success, and begin.

Assignment (Week-3)

Using Visuals

Presentation Objectives

Learn the proper selection of visual aids to support your message.

Gain experience in the use of visuals in your presentation.

Time

Five minutes

Your Assignment

Appropriate visual aids are most often used in presentations where you are informing the audience or conveying ideas of a technical or explanatory nature, such as briefings, sales presentations, or training sessions. Flipcharts, chalkboard, overhead transparencies, slides or photos can help achieve your purpose. Select a topic that lends itself to the use of visuals and plan the speech accordingly.

People believe what they see before believing what they hear; and they remember more of what they both *see* and *hear*. Since your objectives include being believed and helping your audience remember what you have told them, the visual display of your information makes a vital contribution to reaching those goals. Your visuals should convey the meaning of your words and dramatize your speech. They should be simple so that people will understand the ideas you wish to communicate.

Creating Your Talk

Begin building on the outline by planning an introduction that will attract the interest of the group, and point toward development of the main ideas. Among the possible approaches to introduction are:

- A question or statement that immediately brings the group into your talk.

- An appropriate story, illustration or quote.

- A reference to a common human experience.

After your introduction, begin organizing the body of your speech around the appropriate outline. Your goal is to develop three or four main ideas, with supporting visuals in a step-by-step progression. Your listeners will be led to the conclusion you are advocating.

Finally, present your conclusion forcefully. This is the destination at which you hope to leave your listeners thinking. The conclusion should clearly contain the purpose of your speech and stress this purpose in terms of specific responses you want from the group. Strong endings include:

- A summary of points you have made, showing how they add up to support your purpose.

- A definite appeal for action, with supporting material to motivate the action.

- A story, quotation, or example that illustrates the message of your appeal.

Keep in mind that your visual aids are supplementing your presentation, they are not your presentation. If something goes wrong and the visuals cannot be used, you must deliver your message without their help. Here are a few suggestions to keep in mind while preparing visuals:

- Keep visuals simple and uncluttered.

- When in doubt, use fewer visuals rather than more.

- Phrases or words are better than sentences. Be consistent with structure throughout the visuals.

- Use color; it makes your visuals stronger.

- Pause before discussing the information in the visual; allow the audience time to absorb it.

- When the visual is explained, remove it.

- Provide hard-copy handouts to increase audience retention. Distribute handouts after the presentation so the audience is not distracted. If it is necessary to distribute handouts during the presentation, integrate them into the session and leave enough space on the handouts for the audience to make notes.

Presenting the Talk

When you present a talk with visual aids, it is important to remember that a presentation with visuals is forty-three percent more persuasive. Give your audience enough time to absorb the visuals, but vary the pace. If you are using a pointer to show emphasis, put it down when finished.

Now you are prepared to present your visual presentation to your audience. Fix your opening sentence firmly in you mind, take a deep breath and begin.

Assignment (Week 4)

Final Presentation

Presentation Objectives

Plan and organize your speech into a logical message.
Research the facts to support your main points.
Bring together and apply the speaking skills you have learned.
Make a personal evaluation of your progress.

Time

Five to ten minutes

Your Assignment

In working through the preceding assignments, you have acquired a variety of speaking skills and have received helpful feedback from your listeners. Now it is time to put these experiences together into your best effort and evaluate your progress in the program (see the Presentation Evaluation form at the end of this assignment).

Carefully evaluate your strong and weak points in the following areas:

- Your speech organization and content.

- Your presentation delivery.

- How you present yourself.

- How you use your voice.

- The appropriateness and correctness of your language.

After your evaluation, note those areas that need improvement and formulate a personal strategy to turn those errors into strengths.

In this final project, you are asked to use all the skills you have learned and apply them to a well-constructed and well-delivered presentation. This requires careful organization and research to support your statements. Even if you are using the best material possible, your speech effectiveness will be lost if you do not organize it carefully.

For this assignment, select an organizational outline from the two styles listed below that apply to your business or profession:

AIDA

    A — Win their *attention*.
    I — Arouse their *interest*.
    D — Create a *desire*.
    A — Stimulate *action* or *agreement*.

Problem and Solution

1. State the symptoms of the problem to prove it exists.

2. Identify the real problem.

3. State solutions to the problem.

4. Recommend the best course of action.

Creating Your Talk.

Choose a subject that is significant for your listeners. This subject should be represented by a vigorous, lively speech title.

Concentrate your efforts around a specific purpose for your speech. Know how you want your audience to react, and plan the speech toward that end.

With the purpose of your speech in mind, begin research into the subject. You may need information from the library, the newspaper, or someone who is knowledgeable on the subject.

In previous projects, we have not stressed the need for updated facts in your presentations. Now, instead of speaking in generalities and using your own opinions, support your points with specific facts. Once you have collected this information, discard the facts that are not supportive. Use only the information that supports your points. If you include unnecessary material, it will only confuse your listeners.

When either of these suggested outlines is used, open with an attention getting statement. Immediately engage the audience's interest, showing why they should care about what you are saying. Then, in the body of the speech, introduce your arguments. Finally, present a conclusion that calls for some type of action by the listeners, whether physical or mental.

Presenting the Talk

Now you are ready to deliver your final presentation. Fix the opening clearly in your mind, take a deep breath and begin.

PERSONAL TRAINING PROGRAM
PRESENTATION EVALUATION

PRESENTATION ELEMENTS		SUGGESTED RATING			
		Excellent	Very Good	Good	Needs Improvement
SPEECH DEVELOPMENT structure, organization, support material	CONTENT				
EFFECTIVENESS achievement of purpose, interest, reception					
SPEECH VALUE ideas, logic, original thought					
PHYSICAL appearance, body language	DELIVERY				
VOICE flexibility, volume					
MANNER directness, confidence, enthusiasm					
APPROPRIATENESS to speech purpose and audience	LANGUAGE				
CORRECTNESS grammar, pronunciation, word selection					

COMMENTS: _____

_____

_____

Conclusion

My main purpose in writing this book has been to help overcome the fear of public speaking and quickly increase your effectiveness as a speaker.

Learning to speak effectively does not mean just brushing up on articulation, improving your voice, or learning how to plan and organize a persuasive presentation. Becoming an effective speaker does not mean improving isolated skills. It involves the whole you. It means developing a more objective awareness of yourself and how you appear to others. Speaking in public increases self-confidence, and it is this increased confidence that allows you to succeed.

Hopefully, you have learned that good public speaking is not something that is impossible or unattainable. As you practice what you have learned you will know when you are getting better. The signs will be unmistakable. Your audiences will tell you. If they do not, your growing sense of self-confidence will. Confidence is built upon the experience of success. We all learn from experience that we can succeed, and we use our small successes as stepping stones that lead to greater ones.

Bibliography

Berg, Karen and Gilman, and Drew, *Get to the Point*, Bantam, 1989

Burger, Chester, "How to Meet the Press," *Harvard Business Review*, July-August 1975

Clevenger, Theodore, *Audience Analysis*, Bobbs, 1966

Gondin, William R. and Mammen, Edward W., *The Art of Speaking Made Simple*, Doubleday & Company, Inc., 1981

Howell, William S., and Ernest G. Bormann, *Presentational Speaking for Business and the Professional*, Harper & Row, 1971

Jay, Anthony, *The New Oratory*, American Management Associations, 1971

LeRoux, Paul, *Selling to a Group*, Harper & Row, 1984

Linver, Sandy, *Speak Easy*, Summer, 1978

McMahon, Ed, *The Art of Public Speaking*, Putnam, 1986

Painter, Margaret, *Educator's Guide to Persuasive Speaking*, Prentice, 1966

Sager, A., *Speak Your Way to Success*, McGraw-Hill Book Company, 1968

Tice, Louis, *Investment In Excellence, An Application Guide*, The Pacific Institute, Inc., 1983

Wood, Milett, *The Art of Speaking*, Drake, 1971

About The Author

John W. Osborne is a manager of administration with Hughes Aircraft Company, Corporate Headquarters, a subsidiary of General Motors Corporation. He holds a B.S. Degree in Business Administration and a Masters in Public Administration from the University of Southern California. Mr. Osborne is an expert in speech communication and holds a DTM certificate from Toastmasters International. He has made numerous presentations to United States government personnel, corporations and service club organizations. His career includes work in computer systems and administration for companies such as RCA, University of Southern California and Twentieth Century Fox Film Corporation. Mr. Osborne is a Certified Systems Professional with the Association for Systems Management and he provides management consulting expertise and technical training for Southern California companies.